Letters To My Feathered Friends

Observations, Meditations
and
Thanksgivings

By
Tim Stanley

2 Timothy Publishing
Irvine, CA

Front cover design and photo: Ashok Khosla
Photo credits are at the back of the book.

ISBN # 978-0-9842391-1-5
Library of Congress Control Number: 2010903209

2 Timothy Publishing
P.O. Box 53783
Irvine, CA 92619-3783
USA
www.2timothypublishing.com

Printed in USA

2 Timothy Publishing books are available at discount for bulk purchases. See web site for details.

For a copy of this book:
Order online at website above, or send check or money order to:
2 Timothy Publishing, P.O. Box 53783, Irvine, CA 92619-3783.
Shipping and handling are included in the amounts below:
CA mailing addresses: $22.50 (includes CA sales tax)
All other US mailing addresses: $21.00; Canada: $24.00.

Acknowledgements

First, it is most appropriate to give thanks to the One who gives us all things freely to enjoy. What a gift of love birds are! What a display of God's infinite wisdom, goodness and perfection!

Thanks to my wife, Deborah, for her encouragement, support, constructive comments and information technology help, without which this book would not be in your hands.

Thanks to all who granted me the use of their photos for this book. I will always remember the kindness you showed in this endeavor. Surely the mutual love for these friends is a strong and instant bond. Without all of you, there also would be no book.

Thanks to Yahoo!® for their wonderful Flickr® website.

Thanks to editors Ned Nossaman and Charlie Sult, who did an excellent job and were very encouraging along the way. Without Charlie and Ned this book could not have been completed either.

Thanks to our son, James, our daughter, Jennifer, and to Bruce Giddens, Brian Carr, Susanna Chu, Amy Chu, Lisa O'Bryan and John Stanley for their careful proofreading and comments. Without all of you, you guessed it, no book.

This compilation has been a lesson in dependence. A heartfelt thanks to all who gave some technical advice, a word of encouragement, or contributed in any way. May you all, and all who read this book, find the joy I have had in writing it.

Tim Stanley

Preface

Watching birds takes time. They do not reveal their secrets to those who are in a hurry. Yet, "In a hurry" is the way many of us live much of the time. So we miss a lot.

Thankfully, it does not have to be so all of the time, and many of these friends are more than willing to share their lives with us.

Come along with me and meet some of my feathered friends. Some of them you may already know; others you may meet for the first time. All have something to teach us. I invite you to sit back, read this book a little at a time, and consider the birds with me.

Letters To My Feathered Friends

Observations, Meditations
and
Thanksgivings

Contents:

Introduction

The Wake-up Bird

Twee-deet, Twee-doo!
Twee-deet, Twee-doo!
Twee-deet, Twee-doo!

Your piccolo voice echoes down into the house
At the crack of dawn
From your perch atop our chimney.

You're stirring up all the sleeping birds
To greet the day
And sing their praise to the One who made them
And charged them to be His choir.

Soon one joins, and then another—
And sometimes after a while all the air is alive
With beautiful voices singing different parts—
All blending in that festal shout
Of life given for another day.

But sometimes no others will wake up…
Or at least sing.
But you keep on singing.

Thank you, my steadfast friend.
It's a joy to hear you each morning!

Chapter 1: Friends in Our Yard

I have a lot of feathered friends
Who come into our yard for regular visits.

Some are passing by,
Others stay for a season or two,
And a few make their homes here.
But everyone who comes wins my smile.

I'd love to watch you more,
But you've got your work to do and I've got mine.
So we'll take the opportunities we have
And enjoy each other's company when we can.

At least I'll enjoy yours.

The Flycatcher

Perched on a branch of the apple tree,
You're master of all below
And even above for a little ways.
To hunt you need not go far—
A few yards at most,
Once you've taken up your post.

You sit and survey the scene,
Searching your pantry,
Then in effortless grace swoop down
Upon your lunch, catching it in mid-air,
And circle back to resume your watch.
Then do it again,
And again,
Until satisfied.

You can hover too,
And for that I am most thankful,
For thus you dispatch those less desirable folk
Who buzz around and around
And annoy us on the back porch.

The House Finch

Your fiery head tells me who you are
As you go about your business
In the branches of the apple tree,
Picking off the pests for me,
Which for you are dinner.

Thank you, my friend,
You do a great job!

I'm sorry to complain a little, but one of your troupe
Has a habit of sampling all the apples.
A peck or two in each.
Maybe looking for the best one?

Please, in the future, eat all you want from just a few.

I'm thankful you don't do this all the time.
Like the worms do.

I really don't mind sharing with you,
Or with them for that matter,
As you both usually only take a little.
But others I'd like to give the apples to don't understand,
Being used to the store-bought ones.

The Window

You hit my office window hard one day…
Lay still on the patio, all askew.
I thought you broke your neck
And my heart at the same time.

I gathered myself and went out to see what I could do,
If perchance there was some life left—
Or at least keep you from becoming a trophy for the dog.

As I knelt down, you revived
And flew off.
Hope you're okay my friend.

I'm sorry about the glass.
Wouldn't have it there at all
Except that it gets cold in here sometimes.
And that's how I look out.

The Sparrows

"Common" you're called, and so you are,
But not taken for granted here;
We enjoy your company, my friends,
For you our hearts do cheer.

You come onto the patio,
Your mission to gather up hairs
Our dog no more had use of,
So left them lying there.

You stack them neatly in your bill
As we would bundle sticks,
Then take them home to line your nest—
Soft bedding for your chicks.

The carpet yarn you so desired
From the dog's bed proved elusive.
Tug as you might it wouldn't budge,
And this did prove conclusive.

Your mate tried too, to no avail,
And had I come to aid,
You wouldn't have known my kind intent,
But would have been afraid.

So I waited 'til you both left off
From all your efforts grand,
Then went out and cut it off
With scissors in my hand.

Don't know if you ever got it,
Or if the wind blew it away,
But I'm sure you're taken care of,
And in the Father's way.

14

The Starlings

For being so common around these parts
You don't come here much.
But every now and then your troupe
Will drop down onto the backyard lawn
For a snack of seeds,
Then fly quickly off.

Your time is spent in other places,
Like up on the wires by the bike path
Where you perch, all evenly spaced,
And sing your short songs or keep silent—

Whatever the order of the day requires.

The Hummingbird

The high speed hum of a motor I hear
Tells me my flashy friend has arrived.
Seeing me, you downshift and leave your place
Suspended in mid-air
With acceleration that defies
A hot-rodder's wildest dream.

Fiery red hood and silver-green body of glitter paint
Shimmer in the summer sun—
Hand painted by the Master of masters.

You'll take nothing but the highest octane fuel:
Nectar from the honeysuckle bush
Where you built your nest.

Yes, even hotshots like you
Need some time to rest.

The Goldfinch

Ah, pretty little friend,
You take my breath away.
I only get a glimpse of you,
And then you fly away.

One day, a knock at my door.
Two little boys I'd never seen before stood there
With swollen faces and tears in their eyes.
Cradled in the hands of one boy
Was one of your departed brethren.
I'm sure the other boy would have held him
At the same time if he could have.
So great was their love.

I suppose they had heard
Through the neighborhood scuttlebutt
That I loved your kind,
And they asked me if I would please fix their friend.

What do you do in such a case?
What do you say?

I took their little treasure,
Thanked them for their kindness,
Told them I'd do what I could,
And sent them on their way,
I hope a little comforted.

Now it was my turn to hold that treasure in my hand.

I'm writing this so you will know
How precious you are to me.

And to others who can see.

The Blackbirds

I miss you my friends.
For many springs now you haven't come as in former years,
To make your nests in the cypress trees.
The trees are there, but where are you?
Maybe I didn't tell you how much I enjoy your company.

You're honorable folk—
Caring more for family and clan
Than for yourselves,
As evidenced by your labors.

All those years I watched
As you flew down into the yard
To select something to build your house with,
Or to find something to eat.
My, how you work to feed your young!

Your yellow eyes watched me too.
I've wondered what you thought.

I never did anything for you,
Except got in the way sometimes.
And swooping down close to my head
You advised me of my trespass.

When one of your little ones gets out of the nest too early,
Unequipped,
And is lying helpless on the ground,
Unable to fly,
How your clan rallies to protect him!

I don't know if many of these survive
And are saved from the cats and crows,
But your valiant efforts won't soon be forgotten.

The Bushtits

Ah, my wee friends!
So often present but not seen unless spooked.
Then you're all gone so quickly
That we wonder if we'd seen anything at all.

You're a close-knit, secretive bunch.
How twenty of you can be in a small, leafless tree
And remain unseen I'll never figure out.

Sometimes you're quite vocal.
Your soft tones glue all together,
Yet keep each at a respectful distance
As you flit around in a tree.

Thank you for cleaning the alder tree
Of those tiny bugs you love,
Or at least keeping them in check.

I never even noticed them
Until I wondered what it was you were having for supper
And took a closer look after you left.

Thankfully nobody sprayed,
So please come and grace us with your presence
Anytime you want.

The Crows

Sorry my friends, but you were too much.
There were none of you here,
Then you moved in, became dominant,
And drove the others out…
Until the One who cares for His little ones
Thinned your ranks.

We saw you acting strangely weak,
Sometimes with feathers disheveled and thinned,
Sometimes with a ruffled collar around your neck;
And then… here one lay motionless,
And there another.

Now you seem more peaceable—
Humbled and checked by a virus.

Or so they say.

The bags from the fast-food stores
That you summon from the trash cans
Are found lying around the neighborhood
After you've fought each other over the dregs.

You probably shouldn't eat that stuff,
And maybe we shouldn't either.
But we're as lazy as you,
And I suppose as long as we do
And are careless about it,
You will continue.

I like to see you out in the fields
Digging for your grub.
Seems a more noble approach
To making a living.

And I've yet to see a fight among you out there.

The Mockingbirds

Hello, my linguistic friends!
What pretty songs you sing!
All of you have a different repertoire,
Picked up from whomever you listened to.
Oftentimes I'm not sure
Which one of you it is—
Or if it's someone else entirely.

I'm sorry, but at least a couple of my kind
Complain that in their neighborhoods
Some of you have left off praising God
And seem to be more interested in extolling your own virtues.

They say it sounds like clanging cymbals.

Thank you for not doing that here,
But just singing your songs
Because they're in your heart.

Our kind can have this problem too.
I mean, our minds can get puffed up
And we can think we're something we're not.

As if we have anything that we didn't receive.

The Mourning Dove

Good morning Mrs. Dove!
It's nice to see you today!
There you are, sitting on your nest
In the flower basket on the front porch
Where you've come for many years
To raise your family with ours.

Maybe you know you're loved.

When not nesting, you're out and about
Looking for seeds,
Or getting a drink
When someone leaves the sprinklers on too long.

Seems you're everywhere,
Yet you never impose your will on anyone.

When made uncomfortable, you take flight
And with a strong compression of your lungs
We hear your fleeing voice.
You usually don't go far—
Just settle down somewhere else nearby—
As if desiring us to see your graces once again.

You're the meekest of them all—
The offering of the poor,
And shadow of Him to come.

What ails you that you are so named?
Maybe the roughness of a world so unlike you.

The Scrub Jay

You're as bold as the dove is unassuming.
You establish your presence in the yard
And let everyone know who the boss is.

So the others usually leave.

After confidently picking around a little
Under one of the trees,
You're off to go and do the same elsewhere.

You wear the colors of the sky…
But spend most of your time on the ground.

The Grackles

You were the new kids on the block for a while,
Until you moved on, over by the market.

When I first heard you I started,
"What is that?!"
And ran out of the house to see who it might be.

From the neighbor's tree
You were checking me out too—
Not so trustful of this excitable fellow
Standing in the middle of the driveway
Staring at you.

How different are the songs you sing!

And I enjoy them all!

The Junco

For years I called you "Chickadee,"
Your name I didn't know.
Sometimes we think we know a thing,
Then find it isn't so.

I'm glad you like to winter here,
You are a joy to see.
In your black cape you flit around
The lawn or in a tree.

I like to watch you all I can,
'Til duty calls again;
And then I leave with something more:
The beauty of a friend.

The Cedar Waxwings

Majestic, royal beauties!
How stately you appear!
While headed south you ride the storm,
And then you disappear.

Where red berries used to be,
Sometimes there's not one left;
However big your flock is,
Is how much we're bereft.

But don't misunderstand me!
'Tis a small price to pay,
To help you on your journey,
A thousand miles away.

The Swallows

Hello, my swift friends!

Artful hunters in the air!
No pilot could bear the gravitational force
Of your lightning-like turns.
The pull of them is far off our charts.

You build your houses of mud and spit
Up under the eaves at the tops of our gabled roofs,
Or under the bridges that go over the creek—
Precariously perched
With gravity unable to bring them down
Until you've raised your little ones.
A higher law directs your building.

Some of our kind don't like the mess that's left
On the side of the house in your season.
But I think it's well worth it—
To have the pleasure of your company,
To hear the sweet call of your babes,

And to be instructed by you.

The Tanager

You pass through in the spring and fall
Going somewhere I've probably never been.
I'm always delighted to see you,
Especially when you bring your mate.

Your brief visits of a few minutes are cut short
By uneasiness.
It makes me sad that we can't make it
More comfortable for you here.

When you come, your happy colors
Grace the corner of the yard you like the most—
Over by the orange tree.

By the time the fruit is ripe,
You're off to a warmer place.

Do you know that when you're gone
The fruit bears some of your colors?

I'd like to get to know you better,
But we haven't been given the opportunity…

Yet.

The Warblers

"What is that?"
"What?"
"In the tree. There!"
"Where?"
"Never mind. They're gone."

I wish you warblers weren't so shy.
I'm sure there's a place where you find rest,
But it's not here.

You're about as secretive as any we see.
Or don't see.

In the fall I've watched a whole flock of you
Fly into the Magnolia tree out front,
Then walked around the tree to get a better look,
But couldn't find a one.

So we get a glimpse of you,
And that's about all.

But sometimes you sing before leaving.

Thank you my friends.
I can't tell you what that does for me!

The Hawks and Kestrels

We have some others who stop in
For just a little while,
The likes of whom do terrify
The ones here domiciled.

Instantly the alarm goes off—
Cacophony supreme—
All warning with one voice: *"Beware!*
This guy is really mean."

I wish that you would go catch mice
And leave my friends alone;
For this is their own peaceful place,
And one which they call home.

But you make their senses sharper
When you come down in the yard,
For all will band together now,
For all are kept on guard.

I'm not that good a watcher,

There's a lot I do not see,

But thank you, friends, for dropping in

To share your lives with me!

Chapter 2: Friends at the Park

Sometimes we need more space,
And all of you do too.
So though you may not come see us,
We're glad to go see you.

Our evening walks are exercise,
Which, yes, we sorely need;
We've not much time to visit friends,
Or lethargic we will be.

I'm sure you're fine with it that way,
At least so it would seem;
Besides, I'm certain you don't know
Just what "lethargic" means.

The Owls

Hey, little fella with the scary voice!
What do you mean by that screech?

We see you flying seemingly headless,
Silhouetted against the night sky,
And you always get our attention.

Your Great Horned cousin never says anything to us
Other than to ask us who we are,
As we walk past the windrow
Of Eucalyptus trees
Where you both make your homes.

Every now and then a car's headlamps
Catch the snowy show of your other large cousin.
The barns are all gone now,
But his name remains.

I know it's hard on you when we trim the trees,
But trim we must—
Otherwise somebody's house
(Besides yours)
Is likely to get broken up
When the hard winds come in the fall.

I'm sorry we didn't leave you a little more space.
But then the trees weren't here at all
Until our forebears planted them.

Things change my friends,
But not the One who cares for us.

The Killdeer

Ah, my cheery little friend
Whose voice I always welcome,
Though it often means you're
Making the distance between us greater.

It pleases me you don't go far.
Your white undersides glimmer in the evening lamplight
As you fly a short circuit of graceful arcs
Before coming to rest on the park lawn

A little farther away from us.

The Bluebirds

Hello Mr. and Mrs. Bluebird!
What a handsome pair you are!
How can anyone not love you?

We never saw you around here
Until a few years ago
When someone built a house for you,
Put it up high in one of the park trees,
And brought you out for a visit.
Seems you accepted this invitation as home,
And now we see many of your family.

Thank you, whoever it was
Who welcomed these kind, unassuming folks.

The Curlews

When the heavy rains come and soften up the earth,
It's time for you to stop over for a meal or two.
Your long, curved chopsticks plunge past the grass
Deep into the soaked earth with break-neck speed.

What engineering went into your neck and bill!
I don't know that any of us have figured out
The math that Wisdom did in your design.

We saw your friends the Whimbrels and the Willets
Out here not long ago.
They like it here when you do,
In cooler, soggier times.
When the ground holds all the water it can without bursting,
The Diner opens up for all of you.

49

The Accidental

You sang your song so sweetly
That we stopped and just stood there listening.

Found you high in one of the park trees,
Singing out all that was in your heart.

We couldn't move—
Arrested by the majesty of the Almighty
Shown in beauty and weakness.

You had traveled far from your normal range,
So our books call you an "accidental."
A strange term perhaps
For one in whom such perfection is displayed.

No, I think you are a messenger.
And that of Love.

The Gathering

Today was one of those beautiful days at the park—
A touch of fall in the air, but really still summer.

Across the lawn from us a birthday party was going on
With lots of our kind scurrying around,
All talking at once,
And all seeming to be having a good time.

Behind them, at the top of two very tall trees,
Another party was going on.
Some Red-winged Blackbirds were scurrying around up there,
All talking at once,
And all seeming to be having a good time.

I had seen a few of you here a couple days ago—
Here one, there another,
Doing normal stuff.

But not today.
Today was different.
This was an occasion.

I couldn't tell if dinner was provided or not,
But this was primarily a social gathering—
A time to be together, to connect with kin,
And be refreshed by each other's company.

There was a lot of talk,
And it wasn't just, "How ya doin'?" or "Nice day, eh?"
No, today I heard you speak uncommon things.

The variety of songs, phrases, and calls heard today
Was greater than I had heard from you before,
And more numerous than those described in the books
We write about your kind.

I don't know exactly what transpired,
But a lot was communicated.
And I'm sure your clan will be the stronger for it.

The Travelers

Fall is an exciting time of year,
And we always look forward to it.
The temperature is more to our liking
When the breeze comes off the ocean and refreshes the air.

The migrating flocks come too—
Usually in small bands of about twenty or thirty.

Most of you aren't comfortable with our way of living,
So you dart quickly from the interior of one tree
To that of another.
From the covering safety of the trees, you spy out
Where the sprinklers have been left on long enough
To bring out the bugs.

When the table is set and all appears safe,
You pop down for a quick feast,
Then move on.

You need fuel for your journey,
Protection by banding together,
And you need to stay covered
While traveling to your resting place.

Chapter 3: Friends on the Hill

I'm thankful I can go up on the hill to work oftentimes.
There's more open space here,
So I get to see things that I otherwise wouldn't.

There's a whole group of friends on the hill
Who seldom come down to the flats where we live.

I drive up the ridgeline inspecting,
Each time as if it was the first—
Past where the sign for the deer crossing was,
Long since taken down,
As their ancient paths were no match
For our modern ones,
Nor their grace for our speed.

They couldn't fly away as you can,
And though I miss them greatly,
I'm happy to still have all of you.

Good to see so many of you doing well,
Or so it seems—
Even though many of your ancient hills and ravines
Have been reshaped under a grader.

I'm thankful that our kind is learning
To take better care of our charges,
And are more careful now—
At least sometimes—
To leave a little more space for you all.

The Burrowing Owls

Little sentries stand at the sides of their earthen abodes—
Just holes in the ground
Out in the open on the parched floor
Where the scrub brush grows.

I've often wondered how you get along
Down where the badgers and rabbits
And other grounded folk make their homes.

I guess you all work it out.

When I've been in your neighborhood
I've never known for sure
Whose home it was I was walking by,
Or if one takes over from another…

Or who does most of the digging.

It saddened me to see your little colony
Displaced by a wider road.
Hope you found new digs little fellas.

I miss you.

The Meadow Lark

Your happy song so pleasant is,
Your yellow colors too;
You quickly fly from bush to bush,
You have so much to do.

I wish you'd stop for just a while,
To let me watch you some;
For if I'm going to see you,
It's while you're on the run.

The Robins

Beautiful masters of park lawns!
You hunters of renown!

You don't come down to our park in the flats.
The One who determined our boundaries
Prefers that we see you up on the hill.

You hop, hop, hop—and then snag!
How did you know that worm was there?
Who gave you such an ear?

The Roadrunner

The first time we met, you were up in a tree
Just sittin' there staring at me
Looking dumb.

You probably thought I was too.

I got annoyed by you just sittin' there staring at me.
Lacking patience,
And desiring to better understand your name,
I threw a rock toward you to get you to move.
Sorry, I was young.

You hardly budged—
Just kept sittin' there staring at me.
Looking dumb.

I guess by that time you knew I was too.

Since then I've seen you run.
Thanks!

I'd always wondered about those cartoons.

The California Towhee

There you are!
Down in the leaf litter under the trees,
Flipping over spent leaves and bark.

Your browns blend in so well
And you are so quiet we can easily miss you.
Even if we see you, we might not give a second glance,
As you're not gifted with flashy colors.

You rarely say anything when on the ground.
Like other shy friends, your voice is reserved
For flight or for the treetops.

With your unassuming disposition
You appease your hunger and keep the floor clean.

Thank you my friend!

The Downey

You always go to the other side of the tree
Where I can't see you.

We've chased 'round and 'round many times—
I trying to see you,
And you not wanting me to.

So we play hide and seek…
Until I get worn out.

The Woodpecker

Taptaptaptaptaptaptap…
Taptaptaptaptaptaptap.

Hey, pretty fella!
That you knockin'?
Big project huh?

Yeah, I know you don't have time to talk—
Gotta keep the chips flyin'
So you've got a safe place to put the acorns.

I've only got one question,
Then I won't bother you anymore.
I've often wondered:
Do you ever get a headache?

The Quail

Hey Mr. California!
You say everything good about the state
Without mentioning its blemishes.

Who doesn't smile when you're around?
I think you and your tribe
Are the definition of "cute."

Everything you do is wonderful.
Like when you all scurry from under one bush
Across an open space to the shelter of another—
Dad in front,
Chicks in single file,
Mom bringing up the rear,
And lots of times Uncle George
With his family following after yours.

You cautiously look all around,
Then, GO!
Fluffy yellow balls propelled by tiny legs at full throttle—
All as one.

Every now and then one of your chicks
Decides to wander off out into the clearing,
And Mom risks her life to go out and get him.

He doesn't know that he needs to stay covered.
Like we all do.
Because there are a lot of things
That can eat us up.

The California Shuffle

I have one question to ask
Before leaving this lovely place,
And it's for you, Mr. and Mrs. California:

The fast little dance you do in the dirt—
Kick up the dust,
And then peck—
What's that all about anyway?

Chapter 4: Friends Overhead

Many things are over our heads,
Literally and figuratively.

Things too wonderful to understand.

May we never lose our sense of awe!

But if we do,
We have some friends overhead
That we can learn from.

If we'll listen to them.

Soaring Friends

You vultures are the masters of soar!
And, my! What we've learned from you!
Though we have tried with many designs,
On your pattern we cannot improve.

Around and around the hill you go
Capturing the best of the breeze,
Steering with tail-rudder and wingtips too,
And all with incredible ease.

Your gliding play the hawks often join,
Though they must work harder than you;
They're also more picky what they'll take in—
The dump's delicacies they will refuse.

Red-shoulders on street lamps take up their posts
To watch for a blundering rabbit,
Who may wander too far from the bushes,
And should have stayed with his good habits.

Don't see you Coopers nearly as often—
Take a good look when I do.
Your array of colors fascinates me,
And your aerial hunting does too.

Once in a while you Ospreys come in,
Though you never extend your stay.
Less water, "Fish Eagles" seem out of place,
As you soar o'er the scrub and the sage.

With swiftness of flight, it doesn't take much
For you to swing inland, my friends,
And your beautiful browns and whites bless us,
If but for a short while then.

The Kite

"See that bit of white over there hanging up in the sky
Shimmering in the sunlight?

"He's a friend of mine.
Been sent by the Overseer
To keep the mice and gophers in check."

My wife bears with me
Because you and your kind don't always stay
Where we first see you,
And by the time we get a little closer
You've often moved on.
She's a little tired of these wild goose chases
Because her distance vision isn't as good as mine,
And what is detail to me, to her is just a blob.

But this time you stay put—
About forty feet up,
Sitting in the air
Like a Kite.

You've got your eye on something on the ground…

And you're quite patient…

Hovering there…

All you need is a little carelessness below…

And you've got supper.

The Canada Geese

Many a traveling band flies over the house in winter
Seeking warmer climes,
But none announce their presence like you do.

I suppose you make up for
The relative silence of the others
With your un-oiled trumpets.

You work together
To cut paths through the sky
In long "V"s.

If it hasn't rained enough to resurrect the grass,
Or if it's not cold enough, you won't come;
And when it turns the least bit warmer,
You're gone.

You used to come in massive numbers—
Sometimes thousands.
We'd see you in the meadow down by the highway—
A field full of Christmas dinners
Grazing in the tender grass.

Only a few of you stop now,
Mostly at the marsh.
Or sometimes at the parks
Where we built the lakes.

The Gulls

Droves of gulls from all parts inland—
A ceaseless stream high above—
Thousands upon thousands,
All headed for the coast.

Who gave the command
That you should do this all at once?

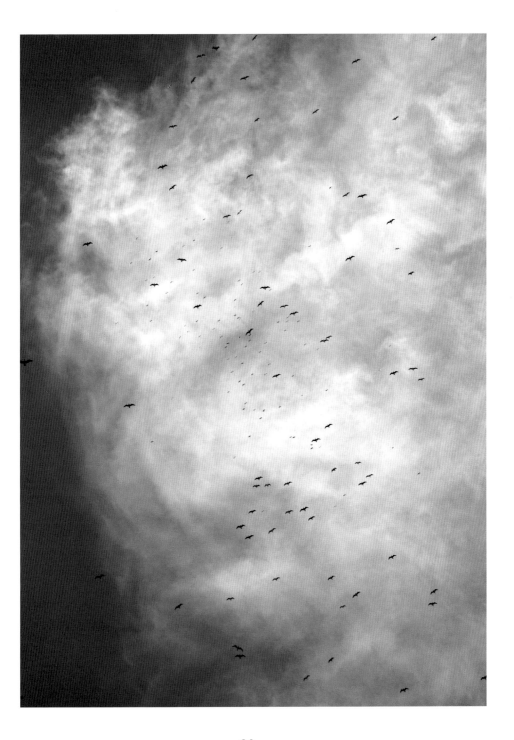

The Red-tailed Hawks

Graceful gliders in the sky,
Circling around way up high,
Just for fun,
Or social time,
Or both.

Sometimes you're a lot lower.

Then things get more serious.
Or so it seems.
Each one who was much higher
Sent down to work his own plot.

Your red tail flashes in the sun
As you circle around.

Looking.

A lizard doing push-ups in the sun
Doesn't see you
Until you're almost on him.

This time he's a little too fast,
So you've got to go up again
And start over.

Looking.

The Dance of Two Armies

A huge flock of shorebirds
Swarms seemingly directionless
Off to the side of the road.

All together you swoop up sharply,
Then quickly to the right,
Or to the left,
Or down again.
But all together,
Perfectly choreographed
Against the backdrop of the morning sky—
Whitened undersides flashing brightly in the sun's rays
As you make your turns.

Cars pull off to the side of the road,
Though many keep whizzing by.

What is this sight—
So striking that people stop
At the beginning of their busy day
To try to gain some understanding?

Some are lightly entertained,
But others take the shoes off of their hearts
Knowing they are on holy ground.

Certainly this dance has some purpose
Other than to cause near-accidents
On busy roads.

Some have suggested that the flock is determining its leader.

If so, it seems like you're being tossed
To and fro by every wind that blows—
That is, by the latest great one who comes along
And proclaims he knows the way.

There never seems to be a lack of these—
Bestsellers of popular wisdom pulling the flock
This way and that,
Leaving the straight course
Etched in stone,
And intended for the heart.

I've never seen a sure conclusion to one of these struggles.
The scene has always moved on past my horizon
So others may wonder at it also.

Besides, my capacity to observe and understand
Is more limited than I'd like it to be.

But even thinking about these displays
Makes one feel quite small.
Humbled by awe.

And I think that's the way it should be.

Chapter 5: Friends at the Marsh

We have many friends at the marsh too,
All with stories to tell
And truth to teach
To any who will listen.

We don't visit here much
Because the sewage is treated nearby,
And sometimes it doesn't smell so pleasant.
But you poor folks have to rely
On what we give you,
And for some of you, this is home.
At least for a while.

We really do our best to make you comfortable,
But there are so many of us
And so few of you.
Now.

Got to bring binoculars out here
Or we won't see much.
Most of you don't let us get very close.
I can't blame you,
The roar of jets overhead,
Of traffic on all sides,
And so many visitors
Makes me a little skittish too.

Most of you stop for a short while
To rest and be refreshed a little,
Then go on your way
To a better place.
I hope.

Don't get me wrong.
I'm greatly appreciative of what our kind has done,
As I'm sure you are—
A valiant effort's been made of late,
But…
It's hard.

The Yellowthroat

You're too pretty, my friend,
To spend your days down in the marsh reeds.

I suppose experience has taught you
(Or maybe it was breeding too)
That the outside is not so safe.

But I think you can't help it sometimes—
You've got to jump up
Out of the bulrushes
And sing.

Thank you, my friend.
You brought me out a little too.

The Marsh Wren

How secretive you Marsh Wrens are!
You are so hard to see!
You might be out upon the path,
But run when you see me.

Your signature, your tail, sticks up,
As 'cross the path you scurry
Into the safety of the reeds—
I wish you wouldn't hurry!

You dissolve into the cattails,
Once in, stay out of sight;
In there you're not afraid to sing,
And sing with all your might!

The Great Blue Heron

Hello Big Blue!

There you are down in the shallow water
At the edge of the pond,
Back-dropped by the cattails and cottonwoods.
Your stride is long, and with every step
Your curved neck juts forward, then aft.

It takes a bit to get you up in the air:
You crouch and jump,
Reach for the sky,
Then with the strength of Samson himself
Your two great wings
Force down the air to lift you up.

Somehow you stay aloft long enough
For the second wing thrust.
You curl your wings in toward your body,
Then extend them up
And eventually pull them down—
All as if in slow motion.

So you begin your flight.

And I marvel every time.

The Night Heron

You surprised me!
Sitting there in your tuxedo,
Long tassel hanging down from the back of your cap.

You were all crunched up,
Perched in a willow tree by the pond—
Red eyes looking at me,
Fearful I was so close.

I was startled too—didn't expect you either—
Certainly not a few feet away.

Outside the marsh we rarely see you at all.
Here, we usually see you at the edge of the marsh reeds,
Basking in the early morning sunshine—
Tired out after working the night shift.

The Grebe

You sit alone with neck erect
Out upon the water,
Paying close attention to what is going on below.

Suddenly you tuck your neck into your chest,
And down you go.

An underwater chase has begun,
Though hidden from my view.

Time goes by as you navigate in the murky pond water
By sight, or hearing, or sonar,
Or maybe something else we don't even know about.

Then you surface somewhere else,
And I can't tell when you've caught your game or missed—
Your poker face always seems to smile

As you sit alone with neck erect
Out upon the water.

The Coots

When you are here, you pretty much take over
At the lakes we've built—
Eat up the grass and make it so messy
There's no place to spread a picnic blanket.

You're a little too successful…
At the expense of others.

But now you're all gone.
Summer's too dry for you here,
So we have a reprieve.

Unfortunately, I've done this same kind of thing myself.
Been too much.
Not thinking of others.
Like the time the landlady told me I could
Help myself to the oranges on her tree,
And I took 'em all.
Oh, selfish me.

Decades later I'm still ashamed when this comes to mind.
And though I made amends
As best I could after the fact,
I still wince at the thought—
And even the more as I'm aware
That the poison of selfishness
Still lies within me waiting for an opportunity.
If I'd take it.

I long for your salvation, O God!

The Egrets

The Egrets fair—Snowy or Great,
Or of the cattle kind—
You wear your white, resplendent robes
And bring pure peace to mind.

Your gracefulness and beauty too
Are always welcomed here.
A ray of hope your plumage is,
Amidst our frets and fears.

Thankfully you don't remain
Within the marsh all day,
But 'round the town where e're we are
Your beauty you display.

I wonder how you can stay white
In all the muck you live in,
And yet you do—to our delight,
A greater secret given.

The Cormorant at the Marsh

I'm sure you didn't know I was there,
Hiding in back of the cattails,
As you sat alone out on the pond.

You looked around a bit,
Probably to make sure no one was watching,
And the next thing I knew
You were standing on top of the water dancing.

You held your wings out like a skirt,
Did a perfect pirouette,
Then flapped your skirt
And settled back down on the water
As though nothing had happened.

But something did.

I just don't know what it was.

The White Pelicans

The flying squadron becomes a flotilla,

The flotilla becomes a dragnet,

The dragnet becomes a dining table,

The dining table becomes

A frenzy.

The Loons

Thought it was a nice place to set up camp,
Out by a lake that bears your name.

We were looking forward to the chance
Of seeing some of you the next day,
But it was already late and getting dark,
So we turned in.

Didn't sleep a wink that night.

It was breeding season
And the loud, high-pitched laughter
Of a hundred lunatics let loose filled the air.

All night.

Maybe you were laughing at us—
The only ones crazy enough to camp there.

But not for a second night.

The Willets

An army marches across the marsh grass.
With intensity of purpose,
Steadily they move forward.

They're hungry,
And eat quickly—
Chattering as they go.

A runner goes by on the path beside me
And the army's banners are unfurled—
A beautiful display of black and white underwings
As they take off.

In a short time they land in a safer place.

And resume the march.

The Mallards

Of all the ducks at the marsh
It's the Mallards, with their lovely colors and blue insignia,
We know best.

Seems you're less nervous around our kind than the others,
And wherever we've built a pond
You figure it's for your enjoyment as well as ours.

You're adaptive and easily tamed.
When bribed.

One of your sisters joined our dog
In the backyard when she was a pup.
And although some training was needed
(On the side of the pup),
The two became fast friends.

Your sister calmed the pup when she was nervous,
As both stayed outside on the back patio all night
When other creatures lurk around.

Thank you, Mallinicious.
We miss you.

Stopping by Ponds on a Winter's Day

Shovelin' Shovelers, sporty Grebes,
Crazy Loons, and Canada Geese;

Teals winged Green and also Blue,
Wigeons, Pintails, Moor Hens, Coots;

Rudy Duck and Canvasback,
Merganser, and big Black Brant;

Buffleheads and Lesser Scaup,
Gadwalls, Mallards, Ring-necked Ducks—

All these grace our ponds sometimes,
All come in from colder climes,
Most don't stay, they're on their way
To who knows where,
I couldn't say.

The Waders

Flocks of waders grace the marsh—
Winter's coming when life is harsh;
All these southward made their way
From northern marshes far away.

The Stilts are there whose legs are pink,
The Avocets with bills do sweep;

Dowitchers bob up and down,
Sandpipers probe bills around;

The Plovers run in starts and stops,
The Yellowlegs are showing off;

Curlews spear with their curved bill,
Whimbrels likewise get their fill;

The Willets keep up noisy chatter,
The Godwits wonder what's the matter.

All these come to wade and feed—
Glad our marsh can meet their need;
Some Avocets and Stilts do stay,
Most all the others fly away.

Chapter 6: Friends at the Seashore

How pleasant is the seashore!
Refreshing to the bone!

And here we have some other friends
Who call this grand place home.

The Seagulls

You are the most common
Of all the birds at the beach.
Graceful flyers
And stealthful liars—
Sneaking up on our picnic basket,
Then looking the other way
As if to say,
"I'm not a thief."

I love to watch you gliding
Above the bluffs—
One going this way,
Another, a little higher or lower,
Going the other way—
Catching unseen drafts
With indescribable ease.

I've never understood that.
I guess that's because we can't see the wind.

Maybe you can't either…
But you sure can catch it.

And not all things real are seen.

The Brown Pelicans

My big friends
Glide so gracefully just above the waves
Looking for fish…
Or maybe sometimes just for the thrill of it.

Ah, but when you spot the fish,
What a show begins!
You swoop up to gather force,
Then go into a dive,
And with wings half spread out to the side
You hit hard—Ker-splash!
Then bob up, very often with your desire achieved.

But you have been made vulnerable, my friends,
For others see your success
And want a piece of the action.
When you surface, there they are
Waiting to steal the fish out of your pouch
Before you can get it down your gullet.

Now you're in a dilemma.
What do you do?
The fish is wiggling in your pouch,
But to get him down the hatch
You've got to point your bill toward the sky
And open it just a bit.
And that's when they snatch.

So you fish for yourself and for them,
For so God ordained to feed you both.
He gives to the just and to the unjust alike.

And sometimes at your expense.

The Skimmer

From above you see the conditions are right,
Then come lower to make a closer inspection.

You circle,
Line up your approach,
And with the swiftest glide,
Perfectly timed,
You agilely skim the water's surface
Dragging your bottom jaw
Into the smooth, unborn waves
To catch your supper.

Who taught you that my friend?

And who gave you such a perfect lure,
That bright orange beak of yours?

The Tweencies

Okay, so you're called Sanderlings.
But my wife calls you "Tweencies,"
And I think that's more fitting.

I hope you're not offended by this.
She says it in love.

It seems your legs move almost as fast
As a hummingbird's wings—
A cluster of little white balls scurrying down
After the receding waves
With needle-like bills plunging into the shiny sand,
Picking up tasty morsels as you go.

When I dig in the sand to see what you're getting,
I seldom find anything.

But I'm glad you do.

The Turnstone

Yep, that's who you are!

The Oystercatchers

The tide is out
And a band of marauders in dark capes
With bloodshot eyes moves in.
Your long, bright red bills gleam like flashlights
In the twilight as we walk by.

Like hungry chickens in a barnyard,
You pick crabs or fish, or whatever you can find
Out of the tide pools—
The crashing waves not bothersome in the least.

You're too busy…

Dining is good tonight.

The Cormorants at the Sea

You stand as erect as a sentry,
Sunning yourself on the rocks.

You've been preparing for another dive
And word has come in from Orville
That the time is right.
He's back,
And he's got fish on his breath.

It takes quite an effort to get you off the ground,
And still more to keep you up.
But under water, O my!
Swifter than a seal you dart by.
The yellow lure of your bill disguises your intent,
As many an unsuspecting anchovy
Has found out.

The Terns

Out over the water there are a lot of gulls today.
But that one is not a gull—that streamlined one
Who darts like a swallow between swift glides.

Your speed and quickness are unmatched by others your size,
And for keenness of eye you have few rivals.

You survey the surface of the water,
Or rather what's below it,
Circle around for another look,
And with fearless speed go into a dive from far above.

And usually hit your mark.

How can you strike the water with such force
And not get all broken up?

I don't understand.

But then there's very little about you that I do.

Well, we need to go home now…

But not before looking out one more time.

The ocean so vast

Speaks of eternity.

And as we watch the ships

Slowly drop off the edge of the earth

We realize that we don't see much.

Chapter 7: Friends in the Mountains

Whenever I need a short reprieve from the bustle,
I head up to the same spot in the nearby mountains.

A half hour drive on city streets,
Another half hour on a bumpy dirt road,
A half hour's walk,
And I'm there.

Sometimes I drive a lot slower,
Or walk a lot slower,
Or both,

To allow my head to un-wind.

Upon arrival I just sit by the creek and take it all in.

And something does get in,
Because I always come back refreshed.

I don't stay long,
But when there I get to visit with some friends
I don't see in places closer to home.

The Flicker

Speckled belly of black on white,
Black stripes on back, on brown that's light,
Red lipstick past your beak does flow,
Brown hat tops off all that's below,
Black tie and tail make you stately look,
As we're together by the brook.

With all these colors, how you hide!
While you search for bugs, flick bark aside,
Up there in the sycamore tree
You're hard at work

And ignoring me.

The Raven

I hear the air being pushed aside
By the powerful thrusts of your wings
As you navigate through the trees,
And recognize you even before seeing you.

You're a picture of strength,
And at the top of your class in intelligence.
Your imposing bill is a warning to all,
And little escapes your attention.

Noah knew what you wanted.
So he let you out first.

Another, seeking life,
Had no rest for her feet.

The Steller's Jay

Hey, Mr. Stealer…
Er, I mean Steller.

In more populated places in the mountains
You're the fearless king of the forest
And self-proclaimed owner of all picnic tables—
Demanding use-tax from all of our kind.

But where few of us come,
You're happy to go about life more peaceably.
At least for us.

I marvel at your bright blue plumage.
Most have coats designed to blend in.
Not yours!
There you are standing out for all to see.

Maybe that's why you're so tough.

The Chickadee

"Chick-a-dee", and so you are,
Your song proclaims your name afar.

You're winter friends around these parts,
Whose cheerful call wakes sleeping hearts.

The ground supplies the seeds you need,
The trees, the bugs on which you feed,

And all seems pleasant when you're here;
Oh, what a way to start the year!

The Dipper

"Who is that down there in the water?
I never saw a bird do that before."

"Looks kind of like a blackbird."

"It's a black bird, but that's no blackbird.
No blackbird does that."

No, you're in a league of your own,
Standing there in the stream having your dinner.

You run around the boulders in the midst of the rapids,
Dipping into the water at your delight,
Picking up delicacies as if at a smorgasbord.

Rushing water spilling over the rocks
Means nothing to you.
If you fall in or get swept away
You jump out and continue on
As if nothing had happened.

Sometimes you dive in,
Stay down for a while,
Then pop up somewhere else.

You are an uncommon delight—
Full of the vigor of life—
Refreshed by spending your days in living water.

The Golden Eagle

Ah! My friend with the renowned eye!
White paint below
Points to your roost above.

But you're not there now.
Gone somewhere—near or far—
Who knows?

You glide across the ceiling of the sky in a straight line,
Covering distance as if it wasn't.

Your nest is near the top of a fir tree
On a steep hillside,
Unapproachable.
And so you are—
Separate from all your brethren.

How different things must appear from far above!
Yet from your height you come down
To be with us…

And by seeing you our hearts rise higher.

Elusive Friends

The Kinglets and the Thrushes,
Spotted Towhees and the Wrens,
The Thrasher and the Nuthatch,
Are also my dear friends.

The Creeper, Hooded Oriole,
The Grosbeak and the Shrike,
Are also found around these parts,
But these I rarely sight.

And if you see the Kingbird,
Kingfisher, Cowbird, please,
Please tell them I am looking,
But them have yet to see.

I think it good to mention
To all of you right here:
You've gotten my attention and
I hold you all as dear.

Conclusion

How thankful I am for each one of you!

For you, my feathered friends,

Who, each in your appointed time and place,

Minister to God

And open deaf ears.

Index and Photo Credits

Listed in order as they appear in the book

Cedar Waxwing	Bill Quinn
Cliff Swallow	Hung Tran
Western Tanager	Bob Power
Warbler (Wilson's)	Jerry Ting, www.jerryting.com
Kestrel	Reinhard Geisler, Florida ; www.reige.net/nature
Park	Tim Stanley
Owl (Great Horned)	Jackie Shulters
Killdeer	~Sage~
Bluebird	Alfred Yan
Curlew	Jim Dory
Accident (Red-faced Warbler)	Amy J. Leist
The Gathering	Bitzy's World in Photography
Travelers	Christine Acebo
Hill	Tim Stanley
Burrowing Owl	Dennis Webb
Meadowlark	Donald Metzner
Robin	Chuck Rogers
Roadrunner, (running)	Nick Chill
Roadrunner, (in tree)	P. Shepard
California Towhee	Donald Metzner
Downey Woodpecker	Diana L. Harrison
Woodpecker (Acorn)	Frank Shufelt
Quail, family	Lee Jaffe
CA Shuffle (CA Quail)	James R. Page, www.jamesrpage.ca
Overhead (clouds)	Brooke Jeffers
Soaring friends	Josh Mazgelis, www.mazgelis.com
Kite (White-tailed)	Lynn Watson
Canada Geese	John Frisch
Gulls, overhead	Alan Grinberg
Red-tailed Hawk	Gene Thompson
Dance	Fiona Elisabeth Exon
Marsh	Tim Stanley
Yellowthroat	Ted Ardley
Marsh Wren	Jerry Ting, www.jerryting.com
Great Blue Heron	James Stephens, www.natureimages.info
Night Heron	Alice Wilkman
Grebe (Western)	Ashok Khosla, www.seeingbirds.com
Coots	Chris Rowell
Egret (Great)	Kevin Cole, www.kevinLcole.com
Cormorant, at marsh	Emily Norton
White Pelicans	Dr. Geoffrey Einon, www.flickr.com/photos/geoff-e